ARCHAEOLOGIST'S
TOOLS

ANDERS HANSON

Consulting Editor, Diane Craig, M.A./Reading Specialist

A Division of ABDO
ABDO
Publishing Company

visit us at www.abdopublishing.com

Published by ABDO Publishing Company, a division of ABDO,
P.O. Box 398166, Minneapolis, Minnesota 55439. Copyright © 2011
by Abdo Consulting Group, Inc. International copyrights reserved in
all countries. No part of this book may be reproduced in any form
without written permission from the publisher. Super SandCastle™
is a trademark and logo of ABDO Publishing Company.

Printed in the United States of America,
North Mankato, Minnesota
092010
012011

Editor: Liz Salzmann
Content Developer: Nancy Tuminelly
Photo Credits: Shutterstock
Special thanks to Dawn Bringelson, Midwest Archeological Center
and Kate Erickson, Anthropological Studies Center, Sonoma State
University.

Library of Congress Cataloging-in-Publication Data

Hanson, Anders, 1980-
  Archaeologist's tools / Anders Hanson.
    p. cm. -- (Professional tools)
  ISBN 978-1-61613-577-5
  1. Archaeology--Juvenile literature. 2. Excavations (Archaeology)--
Juvenile literature. I. Title.
  CC171.H36 2011
  930.1--dc22

                     2010018604

Super SandCastle™ books are created by a team of professional
educators, reading specialists, and content developers around
five essential components—phonemic awareness, phonics,
vocabulary, text comprehension, and fluency—to assist young
readers as they develop reading skills and strategies and
increase their general knowledge. All books are written,
reviewed, and leveled for guided reading, early reading
intervention, and Accelerated Reader® programs for use in
shared, guided, and independent reading and writing activities to
support a balanced approach to literacy instruction.

CONTENTS

DIGGING UP HISTORY

WHAT DO ARCHAEOLOGISTS DO?

Archaeologists dig up many things. They find bones, **pottery**, and tools. Archaeologists study these things to learn about the past.

WHY DO ARCHAEOLOGISTS NEED TOOLS?

Tools help archaeologists do their jobs. Some tools help them dig very quickly. Other tools help archaeologists dig carefully.

ARCHAEOLOGIST'S TOOLS

Trowel

Backhoe

Sifter

Total Station

BACKHOE

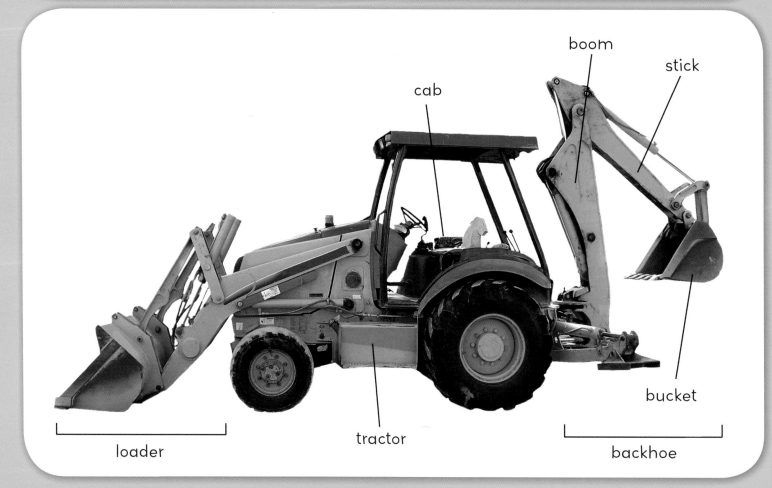

boom

stick

cab

bucket

loader

tractor

backhoe

A backhoe is used to remove the top layer of dirt.

Artifacts can be deep **underground**. Archaeologists use backhoes to **scrape** off the top **layer** of dirt. Backhoes are a lot faster than shovels!

Hunter is driving the backhoe. He is removing the top layer of grass and dirt.

Quinn is digging a deep hole with a backhoe. The walls of the hole show the layers that built up over time.

TOTAL STATION

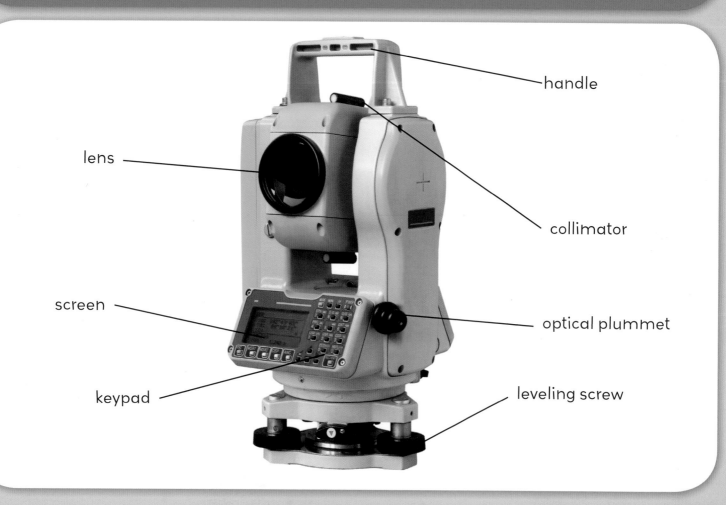

handle

lens

collimator

screen

optical plummet

keypad

leveling screw

Archaeologists use total stations to measure and mark digs.

Archaeologists mark the dig with a **grid**. The total station tells archaeologists where to put the grid lines. It also measures how high the hills are.

Nick is an archaeologist. He uses a total station to measure the dig.

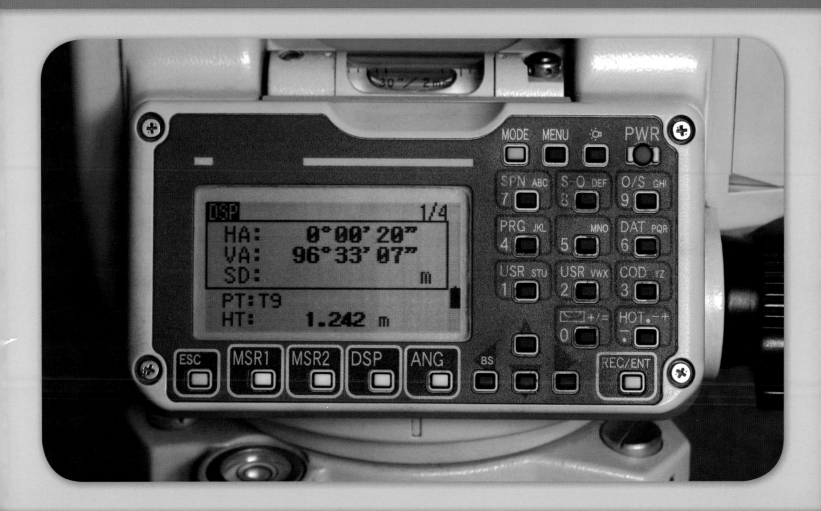

A total station has a **screen** and **keypad**.
The measurements are shown on the screen.

TROWEL

blade

handle

A trowel is used to find objects.

Trowels are small, flat shovels. They are used to **scrape** away dirt.

Sometimes the trowel touches the top of something! Then the archaeologist gently removes the dirt around the object.

Natalie uses a trowel to **scrape** the side of a pit.
She removes a little bit of dirt at a time.

Tessa is looking in the bottom of a pit. She gently **scrapes** the dirt with the trowel.

SIFTER

A sifter is used to separate artifacts from dirt.

A sifter is a shallow box. It has a screen on the bottom. The dirt falls through the screen. Larger things stay in the box!

**Rachel, Chris, and Matthew sift dirt at a dig.
They are looking for small pieces of pottery.**

Paige and Frank use a sifter in an underground dig.

MATCH THE WORDS TO THE PICTURES!

The answers are on the bottom of the page.

1. backhoe

a.

2. total station

b.

3. trowel

c.

4. sifter

d.

TEST YOUR TOOL KNOWLEDGE!

The answers are on the bottom of the page.

1.

Backhoes can help archaeologists work more quickly.

TRUE OR FALSE?

2.

Total stations are used to measure digs.

TRUE OR FALSE?

3.

Trowels are used to dig deep holes.

TRUE OR FALSE?

4.

Sifters do not have **screens.**

TRUE OR FALSE?

TOOL QUIZ

Answers: 1) true 2) true 3) false 4) false

artifact – a simple tool, weapon, or decoration made and used by people in the past.

grid – a pattern with rows of squares, such as a checkerboard.

information – the facts known about an event or subject.

keypad – a small keyboard.

layer – one thickness of a material or a substance lying over or under another.

pottery – things made out of clay and then baked until they are hard.

scrape – to rub something with a sharp tool.

screen – 1. a flat surface on which information can be displayed, such as a computer screen. 2. a framed sheet of wire netting, such as a window screen.

underground – below the surface of the earth.